HATFI**LLD**
AND ITS PEOPLE

THE STORY OF A NEW TOWN, A GARDEN CITY,
AN OLD VILLAGE, A HISTORIC HOUSE, THE
FARMS AND THE COUNTRYSIDE
IN A HERTFORDSHIRE PARISH

discovered and related by
the
HATFIELD W.E.A.

(Members of the Hatfield Local History Tutorial Class of
Cambridge University Extra-Mural Board, organized by the
Hatfield Branch of the Workers' Educational Association, under
the tutorship of
Lionel M. Munby, M.A.)

PART 7

CHURCHES

First published, 17th September 1961
Published with index, April 2014

First published by the Hatfield Branch of the
Workers' Educational Association 1961
Published with index by Hatfield Local History Society 2014
Printed on demand via www.lulu.com

Original text by J. A. Preston
Line drawings by Henry W. Gray
Photographs by Henry W. Gray
Index by Hazel K. Bell
Cover design by Henry W. Gray

This reprint was prepared by members of Hatfield Local History Society
with the kind permission of the Workers' Educational Association.

ISBN 978-0-9928415-6-0

COVER DESIGN

Top: The Parish Church of St. Etheldreda, Hatfield, as it
         appears today (cf. figs. 2-5, pp. 8-9)

Bottom: Brass to Robert Wetheringsete, formerly in Wilburton
         Church, Cambs. He was Archdeacon of Ely, 1411-1444, and
         twice Rector of Hatfield, 1420-23 and 1425-1444, in which
         latter year he died.

FOREWORD

WHEN this series of booklets was published 50 years ago, it was rightly regarded as an exceptionally authoritative and informative work. It has since remained unchallenged as the prime source of reference for anyone interested in the history of Hatfield. Recognising its enduring value, members of Hatfield Local History Society have undertaken this reissue.

Since the booklets first appeared, some of the information contained in them has inevitably become out of date. Hatfield has been affected by sweeping changes, not least by the departure of the aircraft industry and the establishment in its place of a flourishing university and business park. Nevertheless, the original series has stood the test of time remarkably well. We know from our own research experience that it remains immensely useful and we have decided against attempting any piecemeal revision. Instead we have thought it better to reproduce the original booklets without making any changes, except for correcting obviously unintended typographical errors. An important difference is that much more comprehensive indexes have been added.

We hope that the reappearance of the work will stimulate others to undertake new research into Hatfield's more recent past.

Amongst the team who have undertaken the reissue is Henry W. Gray, M.V.O., one of the authors who took part in the W.E.A. class, led by the late Lionel Munby, which produced the original series. The others are Christine Martindale and Jane Teather, Chairman and Publications Officer respectively of Hatfield Local History Society, Hazel K. Bell, who created the new comprehensive indexes, Robin Harcourt Williams, formerly Librarian and Archivist to the Marquess of Salisbury, and G. Philip Marris who led the project.

Thanks are due to Mill Green Museum for allowing some of the original photographs to be re-scanned.

1

"The best adornment of a Church is a numerous and sincere congregation."

2

INTRODUCTION

IN presenting this seventh volume in the series "Hatfield and its People", the editors would like to make some general comments. All the work done by all the members of this group (listed below) is collected centrally and filed. It amounts to a very large number of papers, reports and notes on any matter concerning the town's history, some of which incorporate far more detail than can be published here. As well as written material, we have a large collection of working and record maps, and a fairly comprehensive collection of photographs. All this is available to each author when treating a single subject in one of these volumes, as well as any material that may be collected at the time of writing. In each book we try to indicate our main sources of information. This material forms a historical collection that could be of value to any future historian, or to students engaged in local studies in Hatfield. We have therefore proposed to the County Librarian that we should present the collection to the Hatfield Branch of the County Library when the present series of books has been completed. Miss Paulin has agreed that space will be found to house the collection in the new Library building.

Any reader therefore who has in his possession material relating to any aspect of Hatfield's past, is invited to add it to our collection for the benefit of the town, or if he is not in a position to present it, to loan it to us to have a copy made for the collection. We are thinking chiefly of photographs and pictures, sale catalogues or advertisements, account books or diaries.

The group responsible for these books formed a class run by the Hatfield Branch of the Workers' Educational Association under the tuition of Lionel Munby, M.A., Staff Tutor of the Cambridge University Extra-Mural Board. They are: Mrs. G. M. Brown, Mrs. N. Brown, Mr. S. H. Dawson, Mr. W. H. Dunwoodie, Mr. H. W. Gray, Mrs. B. Hutton, Dr. K. Hutton, Mrs. M. Malcolm, Mr. W. Malcolm, Mr. T. L. Padget, Mr. M. A. Pinhorn, Mr. J. A. Preston, Mr. D. H. Spence.

For this booklet the following sources have been consulted:

i   Surveys of 1534, 1606/7, 1638 and other documents relating to Hatfield Rectory, transcribed in Hatfield Manor Papers.

ii Parish Magazines from 1888 to present day (Parish Church).

iii Scrap book kept by the parish clerk, H. H. Hankin, 1874 (Parish Church).

iv Records of Christ Church, Hatfield.

v   Census of 1851, Public Record Office, and H. H. Hankin's notebook (now lost).

vi   Nonconformity in Herts, Urwick, 1884.

vii   The Church and the Age of Reason, G. R. Cragg, Penguin 1960.

viii   Anglicanism, Stephen Neill, Penguin 1958.

Note: Most unfortunately, the parish records and churchwardens' accounts up to quite recent times are entirely missing, which deprives us of what would have been a most valuable source of information about the daily affairs of the parish. It has been suggested that they were accidentally burned, alternatively that they were lost by a former parish clerk, or again that a former Rector removed them among his private papers when leaving the parish. We do not know, but we have lost a great deal by not having them. This limitation has dictated what must appear as a serious omission in this booklet.

We have been unable to find any evidence to confirm the tradition mentioned on page 8 that the Communion Plate of 1685 was made for the Coronation of James II.

We would also like to thank the following: Rev. J. K. Antrobus, Miss Butterfield, Archdeacon Cockbill, Mr. Elliott, Rev. Gerald Emmet, Rev. D. J. Farmbrough, Mrs. Frankl, Mr. Raymond Gibbs, Mr. Beresford Johnson, Mr. Raymond Lister, Father Milne, Rev. E. M. Norfolk, Mr. Charles Oman, Rev. F. Onyett, Bishop R. D. Say, Mr. J. T. Smith, Rev. J. Stow, Miss Talbot, and, as always, Mr. Lionel Munby.

Published by the Hatfield Branch of the Workers' Educational Association

The Church of England

THE Parish of Hatfield, or to give it its full ecclesiastical name, Bishop's Hatfield, is at present in the Rural Deanery of Hertford and the Archdeaconry and Diocese of St. Albans. In the past the church administration went through many changes.

In the early days of the Church in England, Hertfordshire fell under the direct influence of the Celtic missionary bishops, after which for nearly two centuries (680—870) it was ruled by the Bishops of Leicester. With the Danish invasion of East Anglia the county of Leicester fell and the Bishop was driven from his See; this was then merged into the Diocese of Dorchester and in this diocese Hertfordshire remained for over two centuries (870—1073). The next change in administration took place when part of the county, including Hatfield, was transferred to the Diocese of Lincoln under which it remained for nearly eight centuries. In 1846 the whole of Hertfordshire, ruled then partly by the diocese of Lincoln and partly by the Diocese of London, was transferred to the Diocese of Rochester. In 1877 Hertford-shire and part of Essex were carved from the Diocese of Rochester, and a new See of St. Albans created with the Abbey of St. Albans chosen as the new Cathedral Church.

In 970 A.D. Hatfield was given to the monks of Ely, and their Abbot had the right to recommend ("present") a rector for Hatfield to the Bishop who made the appointment. In 1108 the Bishopric of Ely was founded and endowed with part of the lands of the Abbey, so for four hundred years Hatfield was the property of the Bishops of Ely, from which period comes its full name of Bishop's Hatfield. The advowson of the rectory therefore went to the Bishop of Ely until 1538, when it was conveyed with the manor to Henry VIII. In the valuation of the manor in 1538 the advowson was given a capital value of £40. It remained in the hands of the Sovereign until 1549 when, with the manor, it was granted for a short time to the Earl of Warwick (brother-in-law to Lady Jane Grey). It must have been returned with the manor in 1550 to the King, by whom it was conveyed to Elizabeth. The advowson by this time was considered a marketable asset, profitable because it could be used to fill the vacant living with a member or friend of the family or someone with the desired type of churchman-ship. Elizabeth granted it for a sum of money to Thomas Poyner and William Wolriche in 1563, from whom it was purchased in the same year by Richard Onslow, Speaker of the House of Commons and Solici-tor General. The Poyners, Wolriches and Onslows were kinsmen and belonged to Shropshire families. About 1570 Richard Onslow gave the rectory as a lay estate to his brother for life. In 1574 the advowson was held by Fulk Onslow (Clerk of the Parliament) and 1604 by Edward Onslow, who in the same year conveyed it to Goddard Pem-berton of Hertingfordbury. Goddard Pemberton sold it to the Earl

5

of Salisbury in 1608 and it has remained in the possession of the Salisbury family ever since.

The parish church of St. Etheldreda stands in a commanding position on a spur of high land about three-quarters of a mile from the river Lea. We have no means of assessing the date of the first settlement at the top of Fore Street, or when the first place of Christian worship was established there.

The dedication results from King Edgar's gift of Hatfield in 970 A.D. to the monks of Ely (bk. 1, p. 24). St Etheldreda was the first foundress and patron saint of Ely monastery. Her name was later Latinised as Aldreda and re-anglicised in the middle ages as Aldrey or Audrey, which explains this somewhat unexpected diminutive (cf. Aubrey from Albredus).

According to Domesday Book (1086), Hatfield had a priest who held half a hide, which was a sizeable property.

The first rector whose name we know was Philip de Eya who was instituted in January 1228/9, and after him Nicholas Northwold in 1240. At that time the Bishop of Ely was Hugh Northwold, a very active Bishop who had his properties surveyed in great detail and who is believed to have built a new hall or palace at Hatfield. We must assume that the present Church, dedicated to St. Etheldreda, was built in the early thirteenth century. A relic of an earlier church is now in the Salisbury Chapel; it is a small recumbent figure about four feet long, covered by a shield, it has no name but experts date it as around

Fig. 1.   Interior view of Hatfield Church.   J. C. Buckler, 1839.
(Photo: H. W. Gray, from original in Hertford County Record Office)

6

1190. As Hatfield's oldest citizen, this figure appears in outline on the covers of these books. The Church was in the form of a cross with a tower springing from the transepts; the present thickened east wall and a flying buttress supported this tower. Evidences of early work are to be seen in the South Transept. The reign of Edward I saw the enlargement of the Church by the building of a South Chapel, now known as the Brocket Chapel. The exact date of the building of the Nave is difficult to assign, as in 1871 it had to be taken down to ground level. The present north wall is on the old foundation and the Nave has been lengthened and widened. Much of the material for the construction of the Church came from a chalk pit where Salisbury Square now stands. The flints built the Church; the chalk or marl no doubt proved valuable to the rector for its manurial properties.

The enlargement of the Church came in the reign of Henry VII when John Morton, the Lord Chancellor, was Bishop of Ely. This was the notorious Cardinal Morton of "Morton's Fork". His chief work, in Hatfield, was the building of the red brick Tudor palace, a fine example of early brickwork and among the first unfortified manor houses, of which only the central hall remains. There is much late fifteenth century work in the Church. The tower at the west end is traditionally attributed to John Morton; the central tower mentioned earlier must have been unsafe or destroyed. The Nave was widened and is now out of line with the Chancel; the north door was also erected at this time.

In the time of Bishop Goodrick (enthroned 1534) an exchange was effected between the bishop and the King (Henry VIII) dated 1538, by which lands of the Bishopric which had been sequestered under Henry's anti-monastic policy were restored in return for Hatfield. Motives behind this exchange have been variously interpreted. The advowson of the rectory was then valued at £40.

In the sixteenth century the Church suffered several material losses. In 1506 the entire church plate was stolen by one John Rogers "with force of arms". In 1545 the chantries were abolished and in 1553 all the fittings of the Church were listed for removal. As far as we know, all these rich vessels, vestments and perhaps even the five bells were confiscated by the Crown, except for two silver chalices and two vestments which fell into the hands of Francis Sothwell of Hertingfordbury by the King's gift. In 1590 the fabric of the building was in a poor condition, since the churchwardens were presented in the archdeaconry court for the state of "their steeple and syde beame" and "Ther plumminge and glasinge". A steeple was shown on a map made about 1607 for the first Earl of Salisbury (fig. 2, p. 8).

Pepys attended the Church on October 16th, 1664, and on August 11th, 1667. On the first occasion he saw "Lord Salisbury in his gallery" and on the second heard a moving sermon. The gallery mentioned by

Pepys was situated in the North Transept, the Salisbury Chapel being used solely for burial purposes. The Fourth Marquess who could remember the Church previous to its restoration in 1871, recollected leaning over the front of the family pew or gallery as a child and being fascinated by the flies crawling on the bald head of an old Mr. Webb who sat immediately below, at the entrance to the Transept.

From the reign of James II the Church received Communion plate reputed to be that made for the King's Coronation; this plate, bearing the hall mark 1684, and inscribed 1685, is still in the Church. Chauncy describes the Church in 1700 as being in the diocese of Lincoln and having a tower with five bells. In 1786 the first Marchioness presented a new peal and also a carillon which still plays. Although Chauncy mentions a tower only in 1700, at some time a long thin 'spike' was added to this and is seen on an early eighteenth century painting in Hatfield House (fig. 3). Later than this, in early nineteenth century engravings, a small cupola appears instead of the spike (fig. 4). The bell ringers' chamber contains references to the bells being cast and hung by a "Mr. Briant of Hartford" and opened on June 5th, 1786. These were re-cast and hung and re-dedicated in 1938. The lower gallery at the west end contained the singers and wind instruments until the restoration of the Church in 1871. In this year the fabric was found to be unsafe and a major reconstruction was undertaken in which the Nave was demolished to its foundations. While this was done, the building that now (1961) houses Countess Anne's School was used as a temporary church. The Nave was rebuilt on a slightly larger scale, but a number of fittings, such as the Jacobean pulpit and altar rails, an eighteenth century chandelier and some of the old glass, were thought to be of no aesthetic value, and were disposed of. Some of these have been subsequently recovered. Many old memorial slabs and 'black marble tombstones' were broken up and used as a base for the new tiled floor. James, the Second Marquess, erected a spire in 1847 to commemorate Queen Victoria's visit in 1846. This was a shingled spire and although a great landmark it was never a success architecturally and was taken down in 1930 at a cost of £200, the contractors

Fig. 2. About 1607 (from Estate map).   Fig. 3. 18th Century (from a painting in Hatfield House).

8

also receiving the lead from it, which was of considerable value (fig. 5). Also in 1846, the Second Marquess had some fine cast iron gates made to provide an imposing entrance to the south front of the House. The churchyard gates are clearly by the same craftsman, and incorporate identical castings. Tradition maintains that the gates of Hatfield churchyard were brought from St. Paul's, for which they were made about 1710. If this was so—and it is known that cast iron railings were fitted to St. Paul's churchyard in 1714—those gates have long since vanished from Hatfield, since the present gates were preceded by a simple wooden one.

The Rectors and Rectory of Hatfield

A Parson is mentioned in Domesday Book; he held half a hide, which indicates that the Rectory of Hatfield was from the first well endowed. It seems possible that the Glebe was not in the common fields but a compact holding from very early times, except for six acres, which were divided among three of the fields in several strips. Also belonging to the rectory from times long past when Bishop Hugh Northwold's survey was made, were two minor assets: "the herbage of one ditch (fossatum) near his meadow, yearly rent 3d., and the herbage of one marlpit or delph called Batterdelph, now a large pond, 3d." When these two first appear (1221) it does not seem quite clear what the first represents and it had probably been merged in the Glebe. Perhaps indeed it was the deep gulley of How Dell in which the swallow holes are, which must always have been useless except as pasture.

We may suppose that the first parsons lived in a predecessor of the present parsonage house (Howe Dell Primary School) on the same site in the middle of the Glebe. This was reached from Hatfield by a footpath across the open field of Pittage. The house must then have been like any prosperous farm house of its time, a timber frame house

Fig. 4. About 1800 (from prints and drawings).

Fig. 5. 1872-1930 (spire added 1847).

9

filled in with wattle and daub, probably single-storey and quite extensive but without a chimney, and thatched, with its barns round it for housing the valuable tithes of corn, its fishpond and perhaps a dovecote.

John Taylor, instituted in 1501, was one of triplets presented to Henry VII as a curiosity. Although he was of poor birth this accident secured him a good education, a good living at Hatfield, and several jobs in the diplomatic service. He is known to have been ambassador to Burgundy in 1504 and later played some part in the dissolving of Henry VIII's first marriage. It may be as long ago as Taylor's day that the Tudor dragon and royal lion were painted high up on the wall of one of the rooms of the rectory, now enclosed as an attic. In 1534 he died and was succeeded by William Betts S.T.P.; and on this occasion an estimate was prepared for repairing the parsonage house. This included tiling most of the roofs and flashing them with lead, underpinning and amending the walls of the Hall, "the amending of all the chimnies as well in the backs of them as the hearths; mending the florthes under foot and repairs of windows as well in glass as otherwise." Nevertheless it was still a timber framed construction, very extensive since the repairs totalled £90, though the annual value of all the parsonage house and land with the Tithes was £37. We do not know if the Lord of the Manor or anyone else did these repairs, but Betts died after six months and William May became Rector. He is the first rector who we know let the parsonage house and land, and the Tithes; the tenant was John Kitchen who paid £40 p.a., and this remained the titular value of the rectory until 1607. It seems quite probable that earlier rectors may have let the parsonage and Tithes because there was no compulsion for a rector to reside in his parish and collect his own Tithes: we know John Taylor was often abroad. May later became Dean of St. Paul's.

Henry Bagwell (rector 1559—1584) leased the Rectory and tithes to Fulk Onslow in 1560, whose brother Richard three years later acquired the advowson. This lease, which was for 99 years, was continued by the next Rector, Robert Abbot. Fulk Onslow rebuilt the vicarage near the church for Abbot's successors to live in, but he allowed Abbot himself to live at his own house, 'the Swan', wherever that was.

The Onslows clearly regarded themselves as Rectors by the right of their lease, since they styled the new house next to the Church a vicarage. Fulk Onslow claimed the tithes of Symondshide for Hatfield which had been payable to the Abbot of St. Albans before the dissolution but had been demised for 100 years by the last Abbot to the owners of Symondshide.

In 1606-7 an immensely detailed survey of "all the possessions belonging to the Rectory of Kings Hatfield als. Bishops Hatfield" was made for the Bishop of Lincoln's registry. It is clear from this that the parsonage house formed one face of one of the two courtyards of farm buildings, barns, coachhouses and so on which made up the rectory. This large collection of buildings, including five huge thatched Tithe-barns of five bays each, must have looked like a great farmstead, and was set in an orchard in the middle of the extensive fields of the Glebe (see map Bk. 1 fig. 11 page 18). It is a beautiful situation and must have presented a delightful picture. To this dwelling the first Earl of Salisbury came to live while the new House was being built; he was able to see its walls being raised as he looked across towards Hatfield over the Glebe and the Open Field. A way was constructed straight across the Glebe from the Rectory Gate to French Horn Lane just by the Reed Pond, for better access. Lord Salisbury paid £6,000 for the lease of the Rectory with the Tithes and advowson, and detailed inventories remain of the furnishings he had installed there. As soon as the House was complete, in 1611, the Earl conveyed the Rectory house and lands to his Agent, Houghton, as security for £3,000 in ready cash. Before this, in 1608, Lord Salisbury had made £347.1.11 from the Great Tithes and the rents due to the parsonage. In 1620 the Tithes were leased for £40, the rents amounted only to 15/6d. but the rent of the parsonage house fetched £340: either the loan had been repaid or some alternative capital found to secure it. But in 1626 Luke Rawson paid only £20 rent for the parsonage, house and gardens.

As for Robert Abbot, the Earl was allowing him a pension at the rate of £30 a quarter in 1611, and in addition he derived £15 per annum from small tithes and £13.6.0. from other dues. After paying his curates (Abbot's son and one Samuel Stevens in 1610) this must have left the Rector a rather small income.

Henry Rainsford, the next Rector, held the living of Stanmore, Middlesex, where he resided, as well as Hatfield, and a succession of curates looked after this Parish. In 1646 when Parliament made a stand against pluralities Rainsford was required to choose between his parishes and preferred Stanmore. He was succeeded by Dr. Richard Lee, an opportunist whom some claim to be the original "Vicar of Bray". On January 29th, 1659/60, he preached to Monk's Army at St. Albans but managed to get re-presented to his theoretically sequestered living in 1660 by Charles II. His conduct roused public opinion very much against him and a lampoon poem entitled "The Changeling in the Pulpit", was written by one Wilde about him.

Lee was able to live, in 1657, in a 'few rooms of the Rectory', but it appears that the property had not yet returned into the hands of the Rectors, since in 1650 the value of the Rectory was said to be £450, but the Parson's stipend, formerly only £120, was in this year made up to £200 under pressure from the diocese. In 1652 Mr. Robert Cecil's goods were transferred from Woodside to the Parsonage in two carts: presumably the Parsonage was in use as lodging for the Earl's relatives and guests. In 1670 an attempt was made to raise ready money on the Parsonage lands and a barn by means of an eight year lease for £1,040 down and a peppercorn a year.

By 1719, however, the Rectory had reverted to the Rectors, and Charles Cecil, cousin of the Fifth Earl, is known to have resided there. His arms are embossed on a fine plaster ceiling in one of the rooms. Charles became bishop of Bangor but continued to reside at Hatfield. He has been held responsible for rebuilding and enlarging the parsonage. Probably he merely repaired and redecorated the house and built the fine stable block, for in 1788 when John Keet (2nd) was inducted he found "the Parsonage house, principally built of timber, lath and plaster was . . . very extensive: Mr. Keet pulled down a considerable part and rebuilt the rest". It would be interesting to know just what Mr. Keet pulled down. Much of the front wall of the present building is of timber-frame construction covered with stucco, while the same construction can be traced in various parts of the house and is quite clear in the attics. A comparison of the plan in 1607 and 1960 indicates few major alterations, some of which can be attributed to 1913.

When Lord William Cecil became Rector in 1888, his father, the third Marquess of Salisbury, built St. Audrey's (now a Home for the Blind) and Lord William occupied this as did his successor the Rev. J. J. Antrobus. The Rev. M. P. G. Leonard became Rector in 1936 and returned to the Old Vicarage in Fore Street, and this has continued to be used as the Rectory by succeeding Rectors. In 1954 the present Fifth Marquess conveyed the Old Vicarage to the Church Commissioners and it now became known simply as "The Rectory".

Meanwhile the Old Rectory, as it now became, was sold as a private residence. In 1911 the owner was Archdeacon Gibbs, whose son has given us a detailed account of the building at this time and the alterations made to it by the Archdeacon, which included the beautiful staircase, two small wings at the back, and the present porch. A heavy oak beam removed at this time (1913) was found to have the date 1412 cut on it. It was sawn into planks and makes the present front door. The Old Rectory was purchased by the County Council in 1947 and is now used as a School. It is still a building of great character and charm.

Cecils as Rectors

We cannot here give an account of every Rector, but it is interesting to note that during the past 350 years, while the Cecil family has had the advowson, six relatives of the family have been rectors over a total of nearly 140 years.

Charles Cecil (see above), cousin to the 5th Earl of Salisbury, was Rector from 1719 to 1737. He was later Bishop of Bangor, though he appears to have preferred to live at his Rectory at Hatfield rather than in his Welsh Diocese.

John Keet's sister married the 6th Earl of Salisbury in 1744/5. He became Rector in 1752 and held the living for 11 years.

12

William Cecil Grave was one of the illegitimate sons of the 6th Earl of Salisbury. He was Rector from 1772—1788.

John Keet was the son of the earlier Rector of the same name. He was presented by the 1st Marquess to the living in 1788. This is the Rector who used to give away bread at the Church Door. During his incumbency it is also reported that the Parish Clerk used to emerge from the Church door at the time of services and if, after looking down Fore Street, no congregation presented itself to his gaze, he would return and lock up the Church.

The Hon. William Whitworth Chetwynd Talbot, cousin of the 2nd Marquess of Salisbury, became Rector in 1854 and held the living for 34 years until his death in 1888.

Cussans, the County Historian, has left us his private impressions of this incumbent. He writes:

"The Rectory is constantly under sequestration for the benefit of Talbot's creditors. He and his wife are recklessly extravagant. Being related to the Marquess of Salisbury and being Rector of the Parish, he is, of course, invited to Hatfield House on state occasions, otherwise he has no social status whatever in the County. The last time I saw him he was leaving the tap-room of the Salisbury Arms, smoking a short clay pipe. No stranger would have imagined that he was the Hon. William Talbot, Rector of the Parish, for he bore no mark of his vocation or even of respectability about him; and when he spoke, his profession would be still further doubted".

To make amends for this period Hatfield was blessed between the years 1888 and 1916 with the pastoral care of

Lord William Gascoyne-Cecil affectionately known as "Lord Bill", a son of the 3rd Marquess. He endeared himself to the whole parish by his sincerity and unassuming manner. A contemporary newspaper report describes him thus:

"He was on his bicycle, of course, which he never forsakes in his parish rounds, which cover a large area—I hear he never avails himself of his brother's (the 4th Marquess) cars. Lord William is not an elegant rider and his action on the bicycle is decidedly laboured. He is fond of a slouch hat, a cape that flutters in the breeze and has the proverbial Cecil indifference to clothes.—Lord William is getting more and more like his father.—his stoop is getting more pronounced and his hair is rapidly thinning, but his fine leonine head and tall figure are strongly reminiscent of his famous father".

He was Chaplain to Edward VII and George V and he was greatly missed by his parishioners when in 1916 he was elevated to the Bishopric of Exeter.

13

There are still many old Hatfield people who remember him and his many lapses of memory but all loved him. An old inhabitant speaking of him reports that one of the things she remembers of him is the occasion when he returned after a hard day in London and retired to bed; waking after midnight he remembered that he had promised a sick child that he would visit her and take her chocolates. He at once got up and went to visit the child and take the promised gift. Another memory of this inhabitant is Lord William's interest in China where he made many visits; according to this informant Lord William said that if China was not converted to Christianity in the 20th Century then she would dominate the world.

Among other Rectors not related to the Cecil family, two are outstanding. Francis Joseph Faithfull was first curate in 1812, and then Rector of Hatfield from 1819—1854. He was a man of very strong character and puritanical leanings. He was much concerned with the running of the workhouse, and gave evidence before the charity commissioners about its management. He was also the Schoolmaster of 3rd Marquess (see book 8). Jocelyn James Antrobus, Rector 1917—1936, was deeply interested in the history of the Church and town of Hatfield. It so happened that Mr. Richard Gunton, secretary to the 3rd Marquess, had been engaged on a complete transcription of all papers both at Hatfield House and in public archives, relating to Hatfield. To this monumental work Rev. J. J. Antrobus (as in 1955-7 the authors of this series) had access during his curacy, and wrote the first History of Bishops Hatfield, published in 1912.

In the January 1901 parish magazine, Lord William Cecil wrote an editorial so interesting that we print it here in full as a conclusion to this account of the Rectors.

"January 1901. The New Year.

"In this, our first issue in the twentieth century, we cannot refrain from thinking what changes there have been in our town in the century that is now past and gone. The world was a different world in 1801 to what it is now, and though possibly our town has not changed as much as some, yet it has seen many changes.

"Our town shared in the great changes which have altered the conditions of life of the whole civilised world. In 1800 there was no Great Northern Railway to take you up to Town in half-an-hour, no telegraph and no penny post. In those days rich men drove to London and poor men walked, and did not think much of walking the twenty miles. The oldest parishioner speaks often with contemptuous pity of the modern generation who make such a to-do about walking ten or fifteen miles. When he was young, people walked fifty, and thought nothing of it.

"Then driving along the roads was not as safe as it is now. The guard of the coach was often called upon to act up to his name and defend his charge against some Dick Turpin. It was a much poorer world then. What we now think of as common articles of diet, were then esteemed luxuries. Tea caddies were always kept locked, for the temptation to steal tea would have been too much for many a servant.

"Yes, the world was poorer, working folk sometimes found it hard to get bread enough to satisfy their children, let alone the luxuries that our children are now accustomed to have. The Rector at that date (Mr. Keats) used to give away bread

14

at the church door, but whether that was because he found it hard to get people to church from higher motives or whether it was because people were really in need of bread, we cannot say. How quaint it must have looked to see all the working men walking up the hill in white smocks and york tan gaiters, while the Lord Salisbury of the time walked to church in knee breeches and the Garter ribbon worn over his waistcoat. Though the church was not well attended then, it is related, we do not know with what truth, that the Rector used to tell the Clerk to look and see if anyone was coming up the hill to Church, and if the Clerk could not see anyone the service was omitted that Sunday morning. Perhaps it was this bad attendance that suggested to the Rector the plan of giving away bread at the Church door.

"It was a hard world. Schools were harder. An old lady in this parish relates how when she was a girl she remembers sitting in school while the mistress walked up and down behind the girls with a birch rod which she used freely on the necks of the girls who according to the fashion of the time wore their dresses low. Then prize fighting and cock fighting were not thought cruel or brutalising by the majority of the people. The country was then full of beggars, Irish beggars starved out of their own country, soldiers injured in the war left by a grateful country to beg their bread along the roads.

"Yes, we are richer now though perhaps in some respects we are not better off. We live in a less beautiful world. In 1800 the world was less smoky. We admire now the tints of Autumn, but they are not what they were; our leaves are now all covered with a film of soot, our air is darkened too often by London smoke. In 1800 in the Spring, primroses bloomed in the hedgerows and daffodils grew in the fields, and cottages were covered with thatch, and farmers let their hedges grow and cut them only every six or seven years. Yes, Hatfield must have grown considerably plainer as she has grown older.

"What will this century bring forth? Shall we continue to grow richer and less beautiful? Will Hatfield become simply a part of London? Change is the rule of this world, and possibly A.D. 2000 may see England a land of ruins. The end of this century has found us richer, but has it found us thankful? Have the constant warnings of the changes of wealth been remembered? Will after ages refer to the nineteenth century as the period when England reached its zenith of material prosperity, and its wealth made men lovers of themselves, unthankful, boasters, proud?

"Sufficient unto the day is the evil thereof, and therefore let us put off surmisings and guesses as to what will be, and try to make the present world a happier one".

Other Anglican Churches

As Hatfield parish is so exceptionally large, in the nineteenth century it became necessary to build daughter churches in various subsidiary centres of population, and finally to alter the bounds of the parish.

The first of these was St. Mary the Virgin at Newgate Street, built in 1847 by Thomas Mills of Tolmers (see Book 4, page 23 and cover). This was a chapel of ease to the Parish Church and was served by a curate of Hatfield until the creation of the new ecclesiastical parish by Order in Council of 17th December, 1912.

St. Mark's, Woodhill, was built by the 2nd Marquess of Salisbury in 1852. It was rebuilt by public subscription in 1880 at a cost of £2,000, but is now in the parish of Essendon.

St. John's at Lemsford was built in 1858 by the Dowager Countess Cowper as a memorial to her husband the 6th Earl Cowper who died in 1856. The architect was the same David Brandon who was responsible for the reconstruction of St. Etheldreda's in 1871 (see p. 8). Lemsford was made an ecclesiastical parish in 1859. The advowson of the church was held by the Countess until her death in 1880, and afterwards by her son the 7th and last Earl Cowper. It is now held by Lord Brocket.

Meanwhile in Hatfield Hyde a congregation had grown up for which there was no convenient church. The parish magazine of 1888 tells the story thus: "About forty years ago (i.e. c.1848) the late Mr. Frederick Farr of Woodhall Lodge Farm started a service in his house for the inhabitants of the Hyde. It was felt that a service of some kind was needed, as the Parish Church was quite two miles off from the nearest cottage. This service was conducted by Mr. Stephen Cox, the father of Mr. J. Cox of Fore Street. The kitchen of the farm house was the Church, the pulpit was the copper. In a few years' time the place of meeting was changed and the congregation moved to Pickett's Farm House. Here they were accommodated in the kitchen, scullery and parlour; Mr. Robinson, one of the curates of Hatfield, coming at 3 o'clock every Sunday afternoon to perform service. This arrangement continued until 1861. In that year the late Lord Salisbury (2nd Marquess) built what was commonly called the Mud Chapel. Evening Service was at 3 o'clock, Mr. Farr lending his harmonium which his daughter played. There was no provision made at this time for the administration of either Baptism or Holy Communion. The only piece of furniture in the building except forms for the congregation, was a small desk, serving as Prayer Desk and Pulpit. Some years later, the east end of the chapel was provided with an altar table and altar rails, and Holy Communion was administered on one Sunday in the month. No preacher's book or list of services existed apparently until 1867, the first entry being for August 9th of that year, Mr. Howes being the preacher. It was towards the end of this same year that the font was fixed and there is a note in the preachers' book stating that the font was first used on January 3rd, 1875. Mr. Howes preached on Infant Baptism. It appears that Holy Communion was now administered on the second Sunday in the month at 11 o'clock. It was in this year that a school was founded. It was held in the Chapel, the east end being parted off during the week by a curtain. The only other change was the gift of an organ, formerly in St. Mark's Woodhill, Woodhill becoming possessor of the old organ belonging to the Parish Church."

In 1882, the present church at Hatfield Hyde, dedicated to St. Mary Magdalene, was built by the 3rd Marquess of Salisbury. The architect was Mr. Eustace Balfour, F.R.I.B.A. (nephew of the Marquess). It was opened on July 22nd, St. Mary Magdalene's day, 1883.

16

In the 1920's the building of Welwyn Garden City changed the position of St. Mary Magdalene's from an outlying daughter church of Hatfield to the centre of a new community, and by an Order in Council of 3rd November, 1927, two new parishes were created to fill the needs of the Garden City. St. Mary Magdalene became the parish church of Hatfield Hyde. It was enlarged in 1957.

St. Luke's, Newtown, has a different origin. It was built by the 3rd Marquess in 1877 as a cemetery chapel, but in 1888 regular Sunday services were begun there. The following year an organ fund was started, the Parish being urged to help "the poorer part of the town" (i.e. Newtown) to raise the necessary funds. An organ was installed three months later.

The parish magazine of 1893 reads: "The services have been so regularly and so fully attended that Lord Salisbury, to whom the Chapel belongs, kindly offered to enlarge it. Mr. H. T. Shillito, to whom the task was entrusted, acted on a plan whereby the little chapel of Newtown was converted into a cruciform church, the original part serving as a nave, to which the chancel and two transepts were added. The work, which is done in the early English style, has been admirably and tastefully executed; perhaps the most notable features inside are the dignity of the somewhat short chancel and the open timber roof, which in the centre is carried by curved principals resting on corbals of carved stone". The font was originally in the Wesleyan Chapel. When Mr. Tingey bought the chapel to use as a furniture store, he gave the font to St. Luke's.

St. Luke's now occupies a central position in the town as a whole, and when Queensway was built the appearance of the church was enhanced, being thrown into greater prominence by the new approach. Being convenient to most districts, it is at present a chapel of ease to the Parish Church and a centre for weekday services.

St. John's Church began its existence in the Roe Green Lane "Iron Room" (see Book 2, page 31 and cover). "The Roe Green Mission Room", reads the parish magazine, "was opened on Sunday, December 23rd (1888) when a Service was held at 3 o'clock in the afternoon. The Room, which would hold one hundred and fifty people, is at present only seated for about ninety. Every one of these seats was occupied on the occasion of the first service and several persons were obliged to stand. There was a good congregation again on Christmas Day, numbers of people in that outlying district showing how glad they are to be able to attend a Service without having to walk some miles over muddy roads and pathways. The Room is warm, well ventilated and comfortable, though at present rather bare. A small but sweet-toned American organ has been lent by the Rector, and Mr. Charles Hall has most generously promised to provide a hundred kneelers. We cannot

17

help feeling that such a useful room might be used for many more purposes than to hold a Service once on Sunday. It is hoped that a Sunday School will soon be started there for children at or near Roe Green, and when lamps are provided the Room might be used on weekday evenings as well". The Iron Room was the gift of the 3rd Marchioness of Salisbury.

In 1953 a sanctuary and vestry were added to this original Mission Room, and the whole "tin church" was dedicated in the name of St. John. This work was largely inspired by the Rev. Peter Sutton and the Rev. Paul Goddard, and voluntary labour was used.

In April, 1955, the Cavendish Hall was opened by the Minister of Housing, and a sanctuary at one end of it dedicated by the Bishop of St. Albans; this was used instead of the Mission Room for services. Plans went ahead at the same time for a new church of St. John (see Book 1, cover) at the top of the hill above Roe Green, the highest site in the New Town. The foundation stone was laid by Princess Alexandra on a beautiful June day in 1958, and the church was completed and consecrated by the Bishop of St. Albans on 26th March, 1960. The building was designed by the architects responsible for much of the New Town, Messrs. Lionel Brett, Kenneth Boyd and Peter Bosanquet, and cost £35,000. A free-standing campanile is also planned. Adjacent to the church is St. John's House where the Priest-in-Charge lives. The whole site was given by the 5th Marquess of Salisbury.

From August, 1957, the Roe Green Room has been used for religious services by a congregation known as the Brethren.

Another Mission Room was built in 1890 at Chiswell Green for the people living at Cooper's Green, Astwick, Simonshide and elsewhere in that district. This was designed by Mr. Shillito who later enlarged St. Luke's, and built by Mr. W. Richardson. It could seat 60, and was used once a week for a Sunday School followed by Evensong. This Room had only lasted eight years, when the parish magazine reported: "the old wooden building which has served for a mission room was worn out and rotten, and it became necessary either to repair it or to erect another in its place". The room was pulled down and Lord Salisbury donated a somewhat more substantial, though still timber, erection in its place (see fig. 6). "We can only hope", reads the magazine, "that the parishioners will show their appreciation of the efforts that have been made to provide them with a dignified and suitable place of worship by attending there on Sunday. For, after all, the best adornment of a church is a numerous and sincere congregation.

"We must add that the Mission Room is complete in every respect except the altar hangings. For these we appeal to the rest of the parish since, owing to the poverty of the district and other causes, it is useless to ask the inhabitants of the district".

18

Fig. 6. Chiswell Green Mission Room, now demolished.

The Chiswell Green Mission Room continued in use until the 1930's. During the 2nd World War it was requisitioned and later demolished.

From 1921 when the first houses in Welwyn Garden City were occupied, Rev. J. B. Hunt, who was curate in charge of St. Mary Magdalene, also held services in an old Army hut just off Parkway. Although this centre of worship was not a church and had no parish being part of the parish of Hatfield, in September, 1921, the congregation elected Churchwardens and a 'Provisional Council'. In Feb. 1922 Mr. Hunt died and the following month the succeeding curate, Mr. Hardcastle, held a Public Meeting at which a complete Parochial Church Council was elected and an electoral roll made. This was all in anticipation of a parish being created, which in fact did not occur until 1927. Mr. Hardcastle then became perpetual curate of the new parish of St. Francis of Assisi. The Church of St. Francis was not completed until 1935, when it was consecrated by the Bishop of St. Albans on 18th May.

In Hatfield Hyde parish two daughter churches have been built, first St. Michael and All Angels in Ludwick Way which was consecrated in 1929, and later All Saints Hall Grove, which will be consecrated on 4th November, 1961.

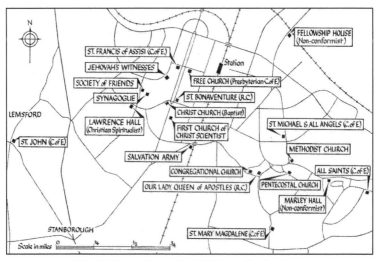

Fig. 7. Places of worship in Welwyn Garden City.

In 1937 in Hatfield a temporary wooden building was dedicated in the name of St. Michael and All Angels on the new Birchwood housing estate. It was intended to begin a permanent church the following year but the War held back this project, and in 1945 it was only possible to build a second temporary church, at the Hopfields end of Birchwood Avenue. This was done entirely by voluntary labour, and was dedicated in November, 1946. The first hut was re-erected behind it as a Church Room.

The present St. Michael's was built in 1954-5 at a cost of £15,000; it was designed by N. F. Cachemaille Day and consecrated on 9th July, 1955. The temporary church now serves as a Church Hall and the original hut has been removed. St. Michael's is a chapel of ease to Hatfield Parish Church, and the priest in charge lives in a parsonage built in 1949 near his church.

20

The establishment of so many new congregations in the nineteenth century was not simply a result of population increase since, except for St. Luke's, none of the churches just described were sited in areas of rapid growth. The state of affairs in Hatfield followed from two national religious movements. First, in the latter part of the eighteenth century the Evangelical Revival recalled the individual to a greater strictness of life, devotion and missionary zeal. Perhaps we may identify the Evangelical spirit, arising among laymen within the Church, as inspiring the early congregation at Hatfield Hyde; and perhaps also the individuals who built St. Mary's Ponsbourne, St. Mark's Woodhill, St. John's Lemsford, and St. Luke's.

Secondly, during the 1830's Dr. Arnold of Rugby called on the clergy of the Anglican church to fulfil their pastoral duties with greater zeal; and from this beginning the Tractarians and the Oxford Movement led by John Henry Newman aroused a great tide of enthusiasm for the revival of Church life in England. Their aim was to restore the full power of the Church's corporate life, and to re-establish regular and meaningful celebration of the sacraments. Hatfield waited long for leadership in this tradition, but in Lord William Cecil was found a Rector not only intensely alive to the religious needs of his parish, but informed with an astonishing energy to satisfy them.

Nonconformist Churches

The Reformation in England, which began as a change in Church government, linked the Church of England to the Crown. From the beginning, therefore, no dissenting opinions could be tolerated, since these would be not only blasphemous but also seditious, and no places of worship other than those of the Established Church were permitted. However, at the Restoration of the Monarchy in 1688 it was clear that the non-conformist sects that had played such a vital part during the Commonwealth could not be completely suppressed. A Toleration Act was passed for licensing the meeting places of Protestant Dissenters, and under this Act over the years eleven such places in Hatfield were certified to the Archdeacon of Huntingdon.

1. "These are to certifie that the house of John Leaper, in the parish of Hatfield, and county of Hertford is appointed and set apart for a place of meeting and assemblies for religious worship by the people commonly called Anabaptists. Witness our hands, James Harding, Hugh Smith, John Hill, John Rawlins, John Adkins, Wm. Woodger. Regd. 27th March, 1694".

2. "These are to certifie, according to Act of Parliament in that case, that a congregation of Protestant Dissenters do intend to meet for worship at the house of Jesper Ireland, of Creamer Hide, in the parish of Hatfield, in the county of Hertford. Witness our hands this 21st April 1701. Henry Johnson, Thos. Ellis, John Land (his mark). Regd. 29th April 1701".

21

3. "This is to certify that we whose names are hereunto subscribed, being Protestant Dissenters, hereby request that a certain house and premises situated in the town of Hatfield, near a pond called Butterdale Pond, in a back lane of that aforesaid town that leads to the Redding road, and the aforesaid house and premises now in possession of a Mr. John Nicholas, baker, may be entered as a place set apart for the purpose of Divine and social worship, according to an Act, etc. Witness our hands this 26th April, 1802. William Broady, minister of the Gospel, Michael Whitbread, Natl. Whitbread, Abraham Jackson, Joseph Broady".

4. "These are to certify that we, being Protestant Dissenters, request that a certain house and premises situated in Tyler's Causeway in the parish of Hatfield, now in possession of Mr. Christopher Gamon, gent., may be registered as a place set apart for Divine and social worship according to an Act, etc., July 19th, 1807. Wm. Broady, minister, Abr. Jackson, D. Hine, John Hedges, John Whaley. Regd. July 24th 1807".

5. "The house of Robert Young, in the parish of Hatfield, certified as a place of meeting for religious worship for Protestants, on November 19th, 1816, by Robert Young". This was Holwell Manor.

6. "The house of Wm. Clarke, in Bishop's Hatfield, certified as a place of worship for Protestants, February 8th, 1827, by W. Clarke."

7. "The house of Anthony Hill, the property of Robert Taylor, in Bishop's Hatfield, certified as a place of worship for Protestant Dissenters, August 22nd, 1827, by Phil. Ellis, John Godfrey, George Hill."

8. "The house of Robert Taylor, in Bishop's Hatfield, certified as a place of worship for Protestant Dissenters, July 26th, 1828, by Phil Ellis, Geo. Clay, Jn. Godfrey".

9. "House at Lemsford Mills certified as a place of religious worship for Protestants (Methodists), on October 7th, 1831, by Wm. Clarke". (There is a Wesleyan chapel here now).—Urwick's note, 1884.

10. "House at Standborough, in the parish of Bishop's Hatfield, certified as a place of worship for Protestants, May 15th, 1832, by Benj. Moorcroft".

11. "The house of John Hawkins, at Bishop's Hatfield, certified as a place of worship for Protestants, December 31st 1832, by John Hawkins and Wm. Edwards (Methodists)".

We cannot tell how many different denominations are represented here, though 3 and 4, 6 and 9, and 7 and 8, clearly relate to the same groups. Nor must we suppose that more than a very small number of worshippers were concerned in any one case. Sometimes a house might be registered simply to legalise holding family prayers.

The first chapel to be built in Hatfield for non-conformist worship was completed in 1823 by the Union of Independents and Baptists. The first register of this chapel was begun in 1836, but it contains a note saying that "the place of worship known as the Park Street Chapel, Hatfield, was built by the Rev. Charles Maslen in the year 1823 and a church was organised by him founded upon the Union Principle". This was a small but simple and dignified building in admirable taste, and it is very unfortunate that it should have survived scarcely more than a century (Fig. 8). Charles Maslen, the first minister, died in November 1829, and after him seven ministers are listed up to 1845.

On his death, Maslen left the Chapel to his wife, who in turn bequeathed it to her two brothers, Robert Young (whose house was earlier registered for religious worship, No. 5 above) and Benjamin Young. The latter before his death purchased the freehold of the Chapel and burial ground and left it in the hands of Trustees for the use of the Church and Congregation. A Sunday School was established in the Chapel in 1831. The first marriage is recorded in 1839 and the first burial in 1846.

In 1845 the Rev. Samuel Raban became minister and continued for nine years until he resigned through age and infirmity. During his ministry the 1851 census was taken, when 328 persons were recorded

Fig. 8. Park Street Chapel, now demolished.

as attending adult services in the chapel on census Sunday. He was succeeded by Rev. Samuel Bird, a Baptist minister from London, during whose ministry it is recorded that the church was blessed with spiritual and temporal prosperity, and many were added to the church. He resigned in 1858 and was succeeded by Rev. T. Crow of London (1858—1862). There followed an interregnum of nearly two years when the church was run by students from Mr. Spurgeon's college, and then one of these, Mr. Joseph Joy, was chosen as pastor. He took up his duties in 1864 and resigned on April 1st, 1871. The register records that Mr. Joy's ministry was a chequered one—sunshine and storm—joy and sorrow.

Another interregnum of two years followed, until in June, 1873, Mr. John Cox Bird "through a remarkable Providence was led to visit this place—he was searching for a place called 'Barkway' and alighted at Hatfield". After four months' probationary service Mr. Bird was ordained pastor on New Year's Day 1874. Mr. John Hankin presented Mr. Bird with a purse containing £20 and also a handsome timepiece. During Mr. Bird's ministry the chapel was reseated and renovated, and the Sunday School enlarged, at a cost of £600. He died early on the morning of Wednesday, June 11th, 1879, after a sudden illness.

The church was then ministered by temporary ministers until October, 1880, when Mr. Sherrell accepted the pastorate. The register records that no minutes were kept, but "the period appears by no means a prosperous one".

In the spring of 1883 Mr. T. Cheeseman of New College was appointed superintendent, but after holding office for nine months declined the pastorate. In June, 1884, therefore, Mr. G. Packer of New College was ordained as pastor, and he served until March, 1892. From then until September, 1905, Mr. G. Garlick was in charge of the church.

The next pastor was Rev. W. A. Buzza who came in May, 1906. During his pastorate many improvements were made to the chapel; it was lit by gas and new furnishings were made. The first World War saw Mr. Buzza on service in France and in the Near East, and he resumed work in Hatfield in December, 1918. After his resignation in 1921 there followed a succession of ministers who held office for short spells.

In March, 1925, Mr. T. W. Lacey, senior student of Western College, Bristol, was invited to conduct services, and made a most favourable impression on all sides of the congregation, especially among the young people. He was invited to become pastor and accepted in May, 1925. He occupied the pulpit as Minister in May and was formally ordained in Park Street Chapel on September 17th, 1925, when it is first referred to as the Congregational Church of Hatfield. Mr. Lacey gradually built up a lively and living church; and as the growing needs of Newtown became apparent, a new chapel became necessary.

A site opposite "the new building site in Stonecross Road and on the St. Albans Road" was eventually bought from Lord Salisbury in September, 1929. Messrs. Spalding and Myers, Architects, drew up plans for a new chapel which were approved in May, 1931, and a tender of £5,456 was accepted for its erection.

The foundation stone was laid by Mr. Halley Stewart, a benefactor, on July 23rd, 1931—the only fine day in a very wet period. There was a service in Park Street Chapel and a procession to the new site. Despite the 1931 crisis work went on and the church was opened on April 28th, 1932, by Sir Halley Stewart. The first Sunday service in Christ Church, St. Albans Road was held on May 1st, 1932.

The last service in Park Street was on the previous Sunday, April 24th. In July the Chapel and adjoining cottage property were sold by auction and demolished. During the demolition a brick grave containing three coffins was discovered: two of them contained the bodies of Rev. Charles Maslen and his wife. They were re-interred in the graveyard. Between two foundation stones was found a copper tablet on which was inscribed:

"This chapel was built by voluntary contributions for the use of a congregation of Protestant Dissenters. The ground on which it stands and the adjoining burying ground was purchased and appropriated to these purposes by the Rev. Charles Maslem of Hertford, Dissenting Minister of the Independent Denomination. This foundation stone was laid and the inscription deposited by him on Easter Monday, March 31st., Anno Dom. 1823".

This tablet is now in the new church in St. Albans Road. A stone inscribed "Park Street Chapel" and dated 1823, which came from the pediment of the old chapel, is now in the wall of the church hall.

A Manse for the Minister was built in 1935. The Second World War saw the Minister mobilised at once, and he was away. The Church and church rooms were used for evacuation purposes, but in October, 1944, the flying bomb which destroyed St. Audrey's School and the Police houses (see Book 6 fig. 7) badly damaged both Church and Manse.

Mr. Lacey resumed his pastorate after the war and eventually resigned in January, 1955. He was succeeded in the following September by the present pastor, Rev. J. K. Antrobus.

Wesleyan and Methodist Churches

Hatfield is bound up with early traditions of the Wesleys. Charles Wesley, soon after his return from America in 1736, visited his sister Nancy, wife of Mr. Lambert, who resided here, and he read prayers in Hatfield Parish Church. John Wesley visited it in 1747, and he preached there in 1772. Other visits are recorded in November, 1786, and November, 1789.

The earliest record of Methodist worship is the registration of William Clarke's house at Lemsford as a place of worship on February 8th, 1827 (see p. 22). At some time before 1851, preaching services were held at a cottage on the way to Sleapshyde. (There is a Methodist Chapel there now). It was here that it was recorded "the vicar of Hatfield (Rev. F. J. Faithfull) did not mind Mr. Raven, the Minister, coming, but he strongly objected to Mr. Wildish, a layman, taking the services". Hatfield Methodists used to go to Sleapshyde for worship. Entire families would go and take meals for the whole day. One incident is recorded of a meat pie which, put on the stove to warm during the service, began to splutter and boil over, to the amusement of the congregation and the discomfort of the preacher, who, however, partook heartily of the pie after the service.

In 1851 Hatfield appears to have had six members of the Methodist Church, and services were begun in "the old cow shed". This was really a very small two roomed cottage with the partition removed, situated at the end of the stable of a public house. (The Two Brewers, see Book 3 page 19). The "Moo-cow Chapel", as it was called, stood at the top of Church Street on the site of the present St. Audrey's Home for the Blind.

In 1864 the number in the society was 18. The Moo-cow Chapel was in use for forty years, while attempts were made to secure a suitable site in Hatfield for a Methodist Chapel. Its dimensions were 14 feet 6 inches by 13 feet six, and "at times the heat was so intolerable and the effluvium from the neighbouring stable so dreadful, it was only by the noblest self-sacrifice that the people had been able to worship their creator there at all". After many weary negotiations a site was obtained in French Horn Lane. The property consisted of two villas with gardens, and a "high" figure of £800 had to be paid, "whereas under more friendly conditions a much less expensive site would have been secured". One of the villas had to be pulled down, the other stands today, and it can be clearly seen where its partner was "sliced off".

Memorial stones of the new church, school and vestries were laid on May 28th, 1889. The "Herts Advertiser and St. Albans Times" of the following Saturday, June 1st, records that Mrs. Camp, laying one of the stones, deposited in a cavity a bottle containing a newspaper and various documents, "but no money". This ceremony was preceded by a short service in the old Moo-cow Chapel before the company pro-cessed to the new site. The new chapel cost £1,200 and was designed by Mr. E. Hoote, F.R.I.B.A. Mr. Thomas Camp of Roe Green gave a considerable sum towards the cost. It was opened on 30th October, 1889.

After this the membership began for a time to increase, from 9 in 1889 to 21 in 1890. In 1897 a resident minister was appointed, but was later moved to St. Albans. For fifty years, up to 1938, this chapel was

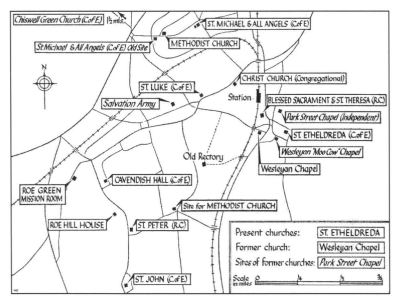

Fig. 9.   Places of worship in Hatfield.

used and the gospel preached against a background of ever increasing
noise from trains. Then it was sold to Messrs. E. T. Tingey and Son
and has since been used by them and their successors as a furniture
store. The congregation moved to a new chapel in Birchwood Avenue,
which was opened on April 28th, 1938. To give some idea of the
growth of the congregation, the number of persons attending services
on Sunday, 15th March, 1959, was seventy adults. Plans are now well
forward for the building of another Methodist church in Oxlease to
be sited near the roundabout in Woods Avenue, which will serve
residents in the New Town. There is a full-time Minister for Hatfield.

The Roman Catholic Church

Hatfield is in the Archdiocese of Westminster, which comprises
all Middlesex, all Hertfordshire, and London north of the Thames
and west of the River Lea.

About the turn of the century Father Kenelm Vaughan, brother of
the Cardinal Archbishop of Westminster, asked to be sent to the most
abandoned (from a Roman Catholic aspect) part of the archdiocese.
The Cardinal sent him to Hatfield. Perhaps the stronghold of the Cecil
family seemed an ogre's castle to the knight errant!

Father Kenelm Vaughan came from an aristocratic Welsh family,
wealthy and with many social connections, and he made use of these

27

assets. At first he lodged over what is now Waters' Garage opposite French Horn Lane. Later he bought a house in St. Albans Road, the site of which is now a car park in de Havillands opposite the Stonehouse. This house he called "Anothoth" after the priestly city of the Prophet Jeremias to whom Father Vaughan had a great devotion. A brick chapel built in the grounds of this house was registered as "A Place of Meeting for Religious Worship" in 1910; in 1911 it was advertised by the promoters of the Nast Hyde housing estate as one of the amenities of the neighbourhood.

Father Vaughan instituted a religious brotherhood named "The Brotherhood of Expiation", to engage in penitential exercises, prayer and active pastoral work in reparation for the sacrileges committed at the Reformation, especially the profanation of ancient churches. He used to enrol tramps and other unsuitable subjects into his brotherhood, very often with unfortunate results. This brotherhood petered out after Father Vaughan's death.

An amusing incident occurred during Father Vaughan's incumbency when his brother the Cardinal Archbishop came to stay with him. Father Vaughan thought it only proper that the Cardinal should have the appropriate ecclesiastical colours on his bed, and proceeded to dye sheets and blankets a cardinal red. The dye, however, was not fast and during the night it spread over the occupant of the bed so that the Cardinal was indeed red the next morning.

Father Vaughan died in May, 1909, and was buried in St. Albans Cemetery.

After his death, Father Kenelm's nephew, Dr. Herbert Vaughan, took over the property for the Westminster Diocesan Missionary Society, of which he was the Superior. There were very few Roman Catholics in Hatfield and the house was let, the parish being run by priests who came at week-ends to say Mass in the brick chapel. In 1922 the property was transferred to the care of Monsignor Henry Barton Brown, who established a house of studies for men wishing to become priests and also for convert clergymen. It was re-named "St. Charles".

At the other end of Hatfield, when the Brewery closed down, a part of the Brewery site was bought by the Carmelite Nuns, who built a Convent next to the railway in 1925. This is now called Silten House, and is a factory for chemical products. The chapel of this convent served as a parish church until a new church could be built, and the property in St. Albans Road was sold. The Spanish Vincentian Fathers at Potters Bar acted as chaplains to the convent and to the parish.

In April, 1929, Father David Arbuthnott, D.D., Ph.D., was appointed to Hatfield by Cardinal Archbishop Bourne. He lived in a bungalow situated behind the block of shops near the present Presbytery. At his first Sunday Mass only nine lay people were present.

Cardinal Bourne bought a piece of land from the Nuns and built the present Church of the Blessed Sacrament and St. Theresa, which he opened on 12th February, 1930. The Presbytery was added in 1932.

The Carmelite Nuns left Hatfield in 1938 and went to Hitchin. In 1959 they moved again to Ware Park, Ware.

Father Arbuthnott left Hatfield in 1933 to take up an appointment in London. His place at Hatfield was taken by a Father Percy Hemus Williams who was an invalid whose health grew progressively worse until he had to spend most of his time in bed, and a variety of helpers came at weekends to cope with the needs of the small parish. He retired in 1943 and died in Brighton in 1947.

On May 19th, 1937, Cardinal Hinsley formally constituted the Roman Catholic parish of Hatfield, and fixed its boundaries as co-terminous with the Hatfield Rural District.

When Father Williams retired, Father David Arbuthnott was appointed to the parish for a second time. He remained in Hatfield until May 1954 when he retired. On 3rd May, 1954, Father Milne was appointed by Cardinal Griffin.

With the establishment of the New Town the number of Roman Catholics grew very quickly. Father Arbuthnott's congregation in 1929 had numbered nine; by 1954 the numbers were over 500, and 544 people attended services on Sunday, 15th March, 1959. In November, 1959, the Cardinal Archbishop of Westminster divided Hatfield into two parishes. St. Theresa's included Hatfield town, Essendon and Northaw, and the new parish of St. Peter, Hatfield South, consisted of Ellenbrook, Roe Green, Oxlease, South Hatfield, North Mymms, Brookman's Park and Welham Green.

In September, 1959, a Roman Catholic Primary School, the Blessed Philip Howard School, was opened in Woods Avenue under the headship of Rev. Mother Mary Carmel, who came daily from St. Albans with other Sisters of Mercy to teach in the school. This provided a centre where Mass could be said in the parish of St. Peter. In October, 1960, a house was found for the Sisters of Mercy in Sycamore Avenue, and Mass was first said there on October 25th. Thus there is a Convent in Hatfield again. Mass is also said in Welham Green in the Memorial Hall for the benefit of the southern part of the parish.

With the division of the parish, Father Stanislaus Savage was appointed to St. Theresa's, and Father Milne took over the new parish. Work started on a Church, Presbytery and Hall at the top of Bishop's Rise in January, 1960. The Presbytery was occupied a year later, and the Sacristy which is in an annex linking the Presbytery with the Church, was brought into use as a chapel in which to say Mass and hold Baptisms and Confessions. The Church and Hall were completed in 1961. The building was financed by a Football Pool started in 1957. Some £14,000 had been raised by October, 1960, a large proportion of which has come from non-Catholics.

On the fringes of the parish two Religious Houses were established between the wars. The brothers Hospitallers of St. John of God came in December, 1930, to Barvin Park, Northaw, where they established St. Raphael's Colony for mentally Defective Youths. In August, 1932, the Dominican Sisters took over Ponsbourne Park, Newgate Street, as a boarding and day school for junior boys and girls.

Can it be that Hatfield is no longer the most abandoned part of the Archdiocese?

Church Attendance

In the census of 1851 a count was made of those attending religious services in all places of worship throughout one Sunday. In 1959 the Hatfield Workers' Educational Association decided to make a similar count under conditions which would compare reasonably with the census. Sunday, March 15th, was chosen, and seven places of worship were brought into the enquiry, with the active co-operation of the appropriate church officers. This is the result as it was reported to the churches at the time.

"REPORT OF ENQUIRY INTO TOTAL NUMBER OF ADULTS ATTENDING CHURCH SERVICES IN HATFIELD ON SUNDAY, 15th MARCH, 1959

1	St. Etheldreda's, C. of E., Parish	361
2	St. Michael's, C. of E., Birchwood	138
3	St. John's, C. of E., Roe Green	102
4	St. Luke's, C. of E., St. Alban's Road	30
5	Methodist, Birchwood	70
6	Christ Church, Congregational, St. Alban's Road	104
7	St. Theresa's, Roman Catholic, Gt. North Road	544

TOTAL of ALL DENOMINATIONS attending Church, 1,349 adults in year 1959.

"For comparison, the enquiry in the 1851 census on Church attendance showed 1,274 'adults' in year 1851 (946 persons at St. Etheldreda's Church; 328 at Park Street Chapel; attending adult services and, therefore, presumably adults).

"The population of the 'designated area' of Hatfield New Town was estimated in March, 1959, to be 18,000 persons, whereas at the census in 1851 there were in Hatfield 3,862 persons.

"Thus in 108 years there was an almost five-fold increase in the population of Hatfield, but virtually no increase in the number of adults attending Church.

"This corresponds to the national figures which showed (roughly) 50% of adults attending Church in 1851, but only 10% now. Hatfield therefore appears to be fairly typical—*so far as these results can show.*"

J. A. PRESTON

PLACES OF WORSHIP

(The address is Hatfield and the denomination C. of E. unless stated)
See Maps: W.G.C, *fig.* 7, *p.* 20; *Hatfield, fig.* 9, *p.* 27.
Dates given in the text are not repeated here.

INDEX

Note: Page numbers in *italics* indicate illustrations.

34

13481393R00025

Printed in Poland
by Amazon Fulfillment
Poland Sp. z o.o., Wrocław